iScier
Reade

New Plants:
Seeds in the Soil Patch

by Emily Sohn and Erin Ash Sullivan

Chief Content Consultant
Edward Rock
Associate Executive Director, National Science Teachers Association

NorwoodHouse Press
Chicago, IL

Norwood House Press
PO Box 316598
Chicago, IL 60631

For information regarding Norwood House Press, please visit our website at
www.norwoodhousepress.com or call 866-565-2900.

Special thanks to: Amanda Jones, Amy Karasick, Alanna Mertens, Terrence Young, Jr.

Editors: Jessica McCulloch, Barbara Foster, and Diane Hinckley
Designer: Daniel M. Greene
Production Management: Victory Productions, Inc.

Paperback ISBN: 978-1-60357-305-4

The Library of Congress has cataloged the original hardcover edition with the following call number: 2011011507

Printed in Heshan City, Guangdong, China.
190P—082011.

Contents

Note to Caregivers:

Throughout this book, many questions are posed to the reader. Some are open-ended and ask what the reader thinks. Discuss these questions with your child and guide him or her in thinking through the possible answers and outcomes. There are also questions posed which have a specific answer. Encourage your child to read through the text to determine the correct answer. Most importantly, encourage answers grounded in reality while also allowing imaginations to soar. Information to help support you as you share the book with your child is provided in the back in the **Additional Notes** section.

Words that are **bolded** are defined in the glossary in the back of the book.

What Are They Doing?

Watching grass grow may sound boring. But grass and other plants have lots of things going on. In this book, you will learn how some new plants grow. You will also solve a puzzle. Plants seem to grow out of nowhere. How can this be? Read on to find out!

Magic Sprouts?

You notice a patch of **soil** in the woods. You pass it every day. One day, you see some tiny green stalks poking out. The next day, the stalks are bigger. New plants are growing in the soil.

You've never seen anyone else at this spot. So, how did the new plants get there?

A new plant is sprouting in the soil!

Here are three ideas for how the plants got in your soil patch:

Idea 1: The wind brought them there.

Idea 2: Animals brought them there.

Idea 3: They were buried under the soil for a long time.

Discover Activity

Many Kinds of Plants

Plants are like children. They need food. They drink. They grow. And each one is different. Let's look at some plants. Go outside and observe plants or find pictures of plants to study. Sort them into groups.

azalea

wheat

oak tree

daisies

How are plants the same? How are they different? Why do you think plants look the way they do?

All fruits and vegetables
are grown from plants.

Did You Know?

How many kinds of plants are there on Earth? Experts have counted hundreds of thousands. People eat the parts of many plants. Common food plants are spinach, oranges, and potatoes. Wheat is also a food plant. Pasta and cereals are made from wheat. What kinds of plants did you eat today?

What Are the Parts of a Plant?

Feet are for walking. Teeth are for eating. Brains are for thinking. What do the parts of a plant do? **Roots** suck up water and food from the soil. **Stems** bring water and food to the rest of the plant.

Some plants have **flowers.** Flowers make **seeds.** And new plants can grow from seeds. Often, seeds become part of a fruit. **Leaves** capture sunlight. They use sunlight, the Sun's energy, to make food for the plant. What would happen if the Sun never shone on your patch of soil in the woods?

What Are Seeds?

A seed is sprouting!
The roots grow downward.
The stem, with leaves on it,
grows upward.

Plant seeds are like chicken eggs. They hatch so that tiny babies can grow. Seeds also store food for baby plants. The outside of a seed is called the **seed coat.** Some seed coats are very hard.

Think about why you wear a bike helmet. Why do you think seeds need coats?

How Do Seeds Travel?

Plants can't walk. But their seeds move from place to place. Some seeds are light. They can float on the wind. Other seeds stick to animal fur. Later, the seeds fall off. Sometimes animals swallow seeds. Later, the seeds come out as waste. What are some animals that eat seeds?

These four pictures show different kinds of seeds.

Puzzle Clue: It doesn't feel windy near your soil patch. But you have seen birds and squirrels there.

How Do Seeds Grow?

Some seeds never become plants. They might sit in the soil for months or years. To grow, seeds need food and water. It can't be too hot or too cold for them.

When the time is right, tiny plants push through the seed coats. Stems grow toward sunlight. Roots spread out underground.

The stem and leaves get bigger above ground. Do the roots get bigger below ground?

Puzzle Clue: It has been raining a lot on your soil. Now it is sunny. You haven't seen animals there in a few weeks.

Why do you think the plants are growing now?

Corn of years ago used to be many colors. The kernels did not always grow in straight lines, either!

Connecting to History

Very Old Crops

Travel back in time 5,000 years. There were no video games, no cars. But people back then were already growing corn. They planted dried corn kernels. Kernels are the seeds of a corn plant. Kernels are the parts of a corn plant that you eat.

Think of the foods you ate this week. Were any of them seeds?

How Do Plants Make New Plants?

Life is a cycle. Many plants grow from seeds. (Not all do.) When these plants grow up, or mature, they can make seeds of their own.

Flowers are the seed factories. First, flowers make a sticky powder. It is called **pollen.** Pollen sticks to another part of the flower, called an **ovule.** Ovules hold eggs. Together, pollen and eggs make new seeds.

Hummingbirds eat a sweet liquid that flowers make.

Sometimes, a seed comes from the pollen and ovule of the same plant. Other times, pollen from one plant travels to the ovule of another plant. Both ways are called pollination.

How do birds and other animals help pollen travel?

Bees move pollen from flower to flower.

One day, you pass your soil patch. There is a flower on one of the plants! A bee lands on the flower. The pollen sticks to the bee. Later, the pollen will rub off the bee onto another flower. That can help new seeds form.

What would happen to flowers if there were no bees?

Science at Work

Beekeepers

Bees don't care much about pollen. They like flowers for their **nectar.** Nectar is a sweet liquid. Bees like to eat it. They use nectar to make honey.

Beekeepers take care of bees. They collect honey from the bees. People eat this honey.

Some farmers get help from beekeepers. They need bees to pollinate their plants.

Beekeepers wear special suits so they do not get bee stings!

Solve the iScience Puzzle

Think about your soil patch. How did the baby plants get there?

Idea 1: The wind brought them there.

Idea 2: Animals brought them there.

Idea 3: They were buried under the soil for a long time.

Think about idea 1. Could the wind have brought the plants?

Yes. Some seeds float on the wind. Your baby plants might have blown there. But you did not feel any wind.

Think about idea 2. Could animals have brought the plants?

Yes. Some seeds stick to animal fur. Some animals leave seeds on the ground in their waste. You saw some birds and squirrels near your soil.

Do you see the burdock seeds on the horses' manes? They will fall off and new burdock plants will grow.

If this squirrel drops a seed, a new plant may grow here!

Think about idea 3. Could the plants have been in the soil for a long time?

Yes. Some seeds sit in the soil for a long time before they grow. Your plants started to grow after it rained, when the Sun came out and warmed the soil.

All three ideas could be true. Maybe the wind blew the seeds onto a tree. A bird ate them. Then the bird left the seeds out on your soil in its waste. The seeds sat in the soil for a long time. Finally, the Sun came out. And new plants grew. What an adventure!

Beyond the Puzzle

In this book, you learned about how new plants grow from seeds. Not all plants grow from seeds. Try this. Grab a potato and a pot of soil. Get help from an adult. Cut the potato into small pieces. Take pieces with "eyes" on them. Put these pieces in the soil, but not too deep. Make sure the soil gets water and sunlight.

After two or three weeks, a new potato plant will grow. Why? Potatoes are plant parts called **tubers.** Each potato piece has a small **bud,** or eye. Plants grow from the buds.

Think about the foods you eat. Could you grow new plants from any of them? What would you need to do to help them grow?

Potatoes sprout from other potatoes. If you put this potato in soil, new potato plants would grow!

Glossary

bud: a new plant, or part of a plant, ready to grow.

flowers: parts of a plant that make seeds.

leaves: parts of a plant that collect sunlight and make food for the plant.

nectar: liquid made by flowers that bees use to make honey.

ovule: part of a plant that joins with pollen to make seeds.

pollen: sticky powder that helps form seeds.

roots: parts of a plant that collect food and water from the ground.

seed coat: the outside part of a seed that keeps it safe.

seeds: plant parts that hold a new plant inside.

soil: dirt where plants grow.

stems: parts of plants that bring water and food to the rest of the plant.

tubers: swollen, underground stems that make buds.

Further Reading

A Seed Is Sleepy, by Dianna Hutts Aston. Chronicle Books LLC, 2007.

The Beautiful Bee Book, by Sue Unstead. Frank Schaffer Publications, 2006.

Eyewitness Plant, by David Burnie. Dorling Kindersley, 2011.

From Eye to Potato, by Ellen Weiss. Children's Press, 2007.

Primary Games. Plant & Flower Facts.
http://www.primarygames.com/science/flowers/facts.htm

Additional Notes

The page references below provide answers to questions asked throughout the book. Questions whose answers will vary are not addressed.

Page 8: Most plants have roots, stems, leaves, and sometimes flowers. They may differ in size, color, and shape.

Page 10: Without sunlight, leaves wouldn't be able to make food, so the plants would die.

Page 11: Seed coats keep the tiny new plants safe.

Page 12: Birds, squirrels, and other animals eat seeds.

Page 13: Caption question: Yes, the roots get bigger underground.

Page 15: Pollen is sticky. It might stick to birds and other animals. Then the animals would move pollen from one plant to another on their feet or other parts of their bodies.

Page 16: Since bees bring pollen from flower to flower, they help the flowers make seeds. With no bees, flowers might not get pollinated. If flowers do not get pollinated, new flowers will not grow.

Index